Rivers

by Alyse Sweeney

Consulting Editor: Gail Saunders-Smith, PhD

Consultant: Nikki Strong, PhD
St. Anthony Falls Laboratory
University of Minnesota

CAPSTONE PRESS
a capstone imprint

Pebble Plus is published by Capstone Press,
151 Good Counsel Drive, P.O. Box 669, Mankato, Minnesota 56002.
www.capstonepub.com

032010
005740CGF10

 Books published by Capstone Press are manufactured with paper
containing at least 10 percent post-consumer waste.

Library of Congress Cataloging-in-Publication Data
Sweeney, Alyse.
    Rivers / by Alyse Sweeney.
    p. cm.—(Pebble plus. Natural wonders)
    Includes bibliographical references and index.
    Summary: "Simple text and full-color photos explain how rivers form and why they are an important landform"—
Provided by publisher.
    ISBN 978-1-4296-5001-4 (library binding)
    ISBN 978-1-4296-5584-2 (paperback)
    1. Rivers—Juvenile literature. I. Title. II. Series.
GB1203.8.S94 2011
551.48'3—dc22   2010002793

Editorial Credits
Katy Kudela, editor; Heidi Thompson, designer; Kelly Garvin, media researcher; Eric Manske, production specialist

Photo Credits
Dreamstime/Alekss, 1; Bynikon, cover, 5; Clearviewstock, 21
Fotolia/Eric Limon, 11; Johnny Lye, 13; rrruss, 15
Getty Images/Superstock, 19
Shutterstock/Adrian Lindley, 17; Fedorov Oleksiy, 7; Pichugin Dmitry, 9

Note to Parents and Teachers

The Natural Wonders series supports national geography standards related to the physical and
human characteristics of places. This book describes and illustrates rivers. The images support
early readers in understanding the text. The repetition of words and phrases helps early readers
learn new words. This book also introduces early readers to subject-specific vocabulary words,
which are defined in the Glossary section. Early readers may need assistance to read some
words and to use the Table of Contents, Glossary, Read More, Internet Sites, and Index sections
of the book.

Table of Contents

How a River Forms

It begins with a trickle.

Soon, a large body of water

flows over the earth.

It is a river moving

with power and speed.

Rivers flow on all continents.

These moving bodies
of water flow
in long channels.

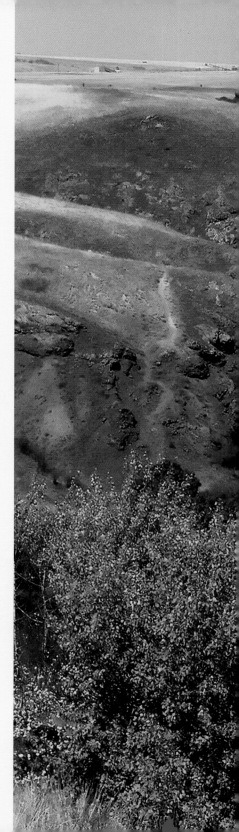

A River's Path

Rivers flow downhill

from their source.

The source of a river is

often a small stream

on a mountain or a hill.

As it flows downhill,

the stream widens

into a river.

Rain and melted snow

add more water.

Rivers can flow

for miles and miles.

But all rivers have an end.

Rivers often flow into a lake,

an ocean, or another river.

Famous Rivers

The mighty Amazon River

is in South America.

It stretches far and wide.

In many places, this river

is too wide to see across.

The Nile is the
world's longest river.
Flowing through Africa,
it is 4,160 miles
(6,695 kilometers) long.

People and Rivers

Long ago, people
settled along rivers.
Rivers made water and
fish easy to get.
People traveled on rivers.

People built towns along rivers.

These towns grew into large cities.

Today, rivers are still

important water highways.

Glossary

channel—a narrow stretch of water between two areas of land

continent—one of the seven land masses of earth; they are Asia, Africa, Europe, North America, South America, Australia, and Antarctica

settle—to make a home or to live in a new place

source—the place where a river starts

trickle—to flow very slowly in a thin stream

Read More

Green, Emily K. *Rivers.* Learning About the Earth. Minneapolis: Bellwether Media, 2007.

Jackson, Kay. *Rivers.* Earthforms. Mankato, Minn.: Capstone Press, 2006.

Internet Sites

FactHound offers a safe, fun way to find Internet sites related to this book. All of the sites on FactHound have been researched by our staff.

Here's all you do:

Visit www.facthound.com

FactHound will fetch the best sites for you!

Index

Word Count: 178
Grade: 1
Early-Intervention Level: 19